The Mint Julep

To Dean Douglass,
who appreciates all
of the traditions of
the Old South.

Love,
Dan

Christmas 1988

The Mint Julep

by Richard Barksdale Harwell

University Press of Virginia

Charlottesville

See here be all the pleaſures
That fancy can beget on youthfull thoughts,
When the freſh blood grows lively, and returns
Briſk as the April *buds in Primroſe-ſeaſon.*
And firſt behold this cordial Julep here
That flames, and dances in his cryſtal bounds
With ſpirits of balm, and fragrant Syrops mixt,
Not that Nepenthes which the wife of Thone,
In Egypt *gave to Jove-born* Helena
Is of ſuch power to ſtir up joy as this
To life ſo friendly, or ſo cool to thirſt.

John Milton, *Comus,*
1673, ll. 667–677

The Mint Julep

WHEREVER THERE IS A MINT JULEP, THERE is a bit of the Old South. For the julep is part ceremony, tradition, and regional nostalgia; part flavor, taste, and aroma; and only by definition liquor, simple syrup, mint, and ice. It is all delight. It is nectar to the Virginian, mother's milk to the Kentuckian, and ambrosia to Southerners anywhere. The mint julep is the subject of the poet and the cliché of the novelist, yet the best receipts for it are more poetic than the poetry it has inspired, and its elusive history is more intriguing than many a piece of fiction.

General Simon Bolivar Buckner (not the Confederate General Buckner but his grandson who was killed at Okinawa in World War II) wrote out, though it was probably composed by someone else, the literary receipt for the twentieth-century julep. Here are General Buckner's directions for the "Mint Julep—the quintessence of gentlemanly beverages" as he recorded them in a letter to a fellow general:

A Mint Julep is not the product of a formula—it is a ceremony and must be performed by a gentleman possessing a true sense of the artistic, a deep reverence for the ingredients and a proper appreciation of the occasion. It is a *rite* that must not be entrusted to a novice, a statistician nor a Yankee. It is a heritage of the Old South, an emblem of hospitality and a vehicle in which noble minds can travel together upon the flowerstrewn paths of a happy and congenial thought.

So far as the mere mechanics of the operation are concerned, the procedure, stripped of its ceremonial embellishments, can be described as follows—

Go to a spring where cool, crystal-clear water bubbles from under a bank of dew-washed ferns. In a consecrated vessel dip up a little water at the source.

Follow the stream through its banks of green moss and wild flowers until it broadens and trickles through beds of mint growing in aromatic profusion and waving softly in the summer breeze. Gather the sweetest and tenderest shoots and gently carry them home. Go to the sideboard and select a decanter of Kentucky Bourbon distilled by a master hand, mellowed with age yet still vigorous and inspiring. An ancestral sugar bowl, a row of silver goblets, some spoons and some ice and you are ready to start.

Into a canvas bag, pound twice as much ice as you think you will need. Make it fine as snow, and keep it dry and do not allow it to degenerate into slush.

Into each goblet put a slightly heaping teaspoonful of granulated sugar, barely cover this with spring water and slightly bruise one mint leaf into this, leaving the spoon in the goblet. Then pour elixir from the decanter until the goblets are about one-fourth full. Fill the goblets with snow ice, sprinkling in a small amount of sugar as you fill. Wipe the outside of the goblets dry and embellish copiously with mint.

Then comes the important and delicate operation of

frosting. By proper manipulation of the spoon the ingredients are circulated and blended until nature, wishing to take a further hand and add another of its beautiful phenomena, encrusts the whole in a glistening coat of white frost. Thus harmoniously blended by the deft touches of a skilled hand, you have a beverage eminently appropriate for honorable men and beautiful women.

When all is ready assemble your guests on the porch or in the garden where the aroma of the juleps will rise Heavenward and make the birds sing.

Propose a worthy toast, raise the goblet to your lips, bury your nose in the mint, inhale a deep breath of its fragrance and sip the nectar of the gods.

Being overcome by thirst I can write no further.[1]

Buckner's is the post-prohibition mint julep, and very different it is from its pre–Civil War ancestors. An article by Theodore Irwin declares that the mint julep's origin "has never been traced."[2] While the identity of the drinker who first put "greens in his whiskey" is forever lost to history, there is sufficient record to identify roughly where and roughly when the mint julep made its first appearance and plenty of evidence to trace its permutations over nearly two centuries.

That greatest of reference books, *The Oxford English Dictionary*, traces the origin of the word "julep" to the Arabic *julab* or Persian *gul-ab*: "rose-water." The word was adapted into most of the western European languages, as *julep* in French and Proven-

3

çal, *julepe* in Portuguese and Spanish, and *giulebbe* or *giulebbo* in Italian. It is cited as occurring in English as early as 1400 and indicating "a sirup made only of water and sugar." Its use in this meaning was primarily medical, but by the seventeenth century the word was used also to describe a sweet concoction drunk for pleasure. Milton used it thus in *Comus*:

> Behold this cordial Julep here
> That flames, and dances in his crystal bounds
> With spirits of balm, and fragrant Syrops mixt,[3]

which might, indeed, be a very good description of the mint julep but was not so intended.

The mint julep is truly American in its origin. A plainer julep is mentioned in *The American Museum* of 1787. This mention establishes as very early the tradition of the julep as a draught with which to start the day. The *Museum* describes the routine of the Virginian as that of one who rises about six o'clock and then "drinks a julep made of rum, water, and sugar, but very strong."[4] In John Davis's *Travels of Four Years and a Half in the United States of America . . .* , first published in London in 1803,[5] is the earliest record of mint as an ingredient of the julep. Davis, an Englishman, was tutor on a plantation in northern Virginia. He became friendly with one of his employer's slaves, a Negro called Dick. Davis recorded Dick's story, ostensibly in the Negro's own words:

4

" 'Squire *Sutherland* had a son who rode every fall to look at a plantation on *James River*, which was under the care of an overseer. Young master could not go without somebody on another horse to carry his saddle-bags, and I was made his groom.

"This young chap, Sir, (here *Dick* winked his left eye,) was a trimmer. The first thing he did on getting out of bed was to call for a *Julep*; and I honestly date my own love of whiskey from mixing and tasting my young master's juleps."[6]

In a footnote Davis defines "julep" for the benefit of his English readers: "A dram of spirituous liquor that has mint in it, taken by *Virginians* of a morning."[7]

Such a felicitous custom was not likely to go unemulated, certainly not in the America of the Federal period, where drinking was a commonplace of everyday life. Americans of the early Republic drank with more gusto than discernment. Sarah Porter Hillhouse wrote to her father in South Hadley, Massachusetts, in 1787 from the frontier town of Washington, Georgia:

There are a few, and a very few, Worthy good people in the Country, near us, but the people in general are the most prophane, blasphemous set of people I ever heard of. They make it a steady practice (if they have money) to come to town every day if possible, and as Mr. Hillhouse is the only person that keeps Liquors, we have the whole throng around us, as many as fifty at a time, take one day with another, and sometimes when any public business is done, which is often, fourteen or sixteen hundred standing so thick that they look like a flock of Blackbirds, and perhaps not one in fifty but what we call fighting drunk. . . . They have spent in our cellar for liquor in one day Thirty Pounds Stg., and not a drop carried 1 rod from the store, but sit on a log and swallow it as quickly as possible.[8]

Gerald Carson in his *Rum and Reform in Old New England* notes:

Per capita consumption figures tell a significant story and forecast the reaction that was swiftly coming. In 1792 the average per capita consumption in the United States was about two and a half gallons of spirits, a figure which included women, children, slaves, and Indians. In 1810 the figure had risen to four and four-sevenths gallons, according to Samuel Dexter, who had been both Secretary of War and of the Treasury during the administration of John Adams and who was then President of the Massachusetts Society for the Suppression of Intemperance. In 1823 consumption had risen to seven and a half gallons, and Dudley, Massachusetts, topped out in 1826 with a peak figure of ten gallons per head. As Dexter put it, sadly: "The pocket-flask is grown into a case-bottle, and the keg into a barrel."[9]

In a paper on temperance written for presentation to the Georgia Medical Society about 1832 Dr. William R. Waring of Savannah described the gustatory habits of the inhabitants of that aristocratic city. Concerning drinking he said:

The drink is very rarely of pure water; it is either a compound of brandy and water or of strong Madeira wine. The quantity taken is various according to the characters of the individuals, but in many instances it is undoubtedly very considerable. It is customary to invite guests who call on a Gentleman at any period of the day and especially at mid-day, to refresh themselves with brandy and water or with wine. It is a civility establish'd by Society. From 12 o'c until the hour of bedtime it is usual for a great portion of the population, not the female of course, to resort more or less to these articles. . . . There are many unquestionably who commence the business of inflammatory potations at a very early hour in the morning before breakfast. . . .

Throughout the United States potations of alcoholic beverages in some form are indulged in with an astounding and ruinous freedom. The very rich take Madeira wine which contains one part in six of alcohol. Those in comfortable circumstances use Brandy, and the Poor or laboring class of people drink the domestic liquor call'd whiskey. With the inhabitants of Savannah whiskey is not in current use. Whether it be owing to the despotism of custom or to the enfeebling impression of the Climate or to both, it is not perhaps very easy to decide, but it is certain that the propensity to excess among us is very great. It is the curse of our community.[10]

The forces of temperance eventually made great gains. The progress of the movement is widely documented. Unusual, perhaps unique, however, is the report of the meeting of an Anti-Temperance Society that Charles Joseph Latrobe recorded as occurring in Tallahassee, Florida, in the spring of 1833. The meeting was proclaimed in reaction against the "attempt of a number of well-meaning inhabitants to institute a Temperance Society." "Great disorder prevailed, and the mouths of the advocates in favor of the Society peremptorily closed." In preparation for the meeting of the Anti-Temperance Society "Captain B., our hotel-keeper," wrote Latrobe, "immediately came forward in the most handsome manner, and offered the use of his great room for the occasion. How public spirited! I observed that an extra hundred clean tumblers were slily got ready within the bar, in case of their being by any chance needed."[11]

Latrobe's account continues:

From the number enrolled under the banners of the Anti-Temperance Society, their general character—and their continual appearance at the bar, where the Captain and his aids were kept incessantly busy for some hours, preparing tumblers of mint-julep, it might be surmised, without any reference to the proceedings within, that the cause of Temperance had, as yet, but few backers in Tallahassee. One or two stout-hearted advocates who stood up in the room . . . were silenced by acclamation. . . .

As to the rest, it was agreed by the majority of the good people of Tallahassee, to go on drinking and stimulating with mint-julep, mint sling, bitters, hail-stone, snow-storm, apple-toddy, punch, Tom and Jerry, egg-nogg—and to remain dram-drinkers and tipplers, if not absolute drunkards, in spite of the machinations of the Temperance men.[12]

Here Latrobe dilated on the mint julep and its charms:

And pray, what is mint-julep? I hear you ask. I've got the receipt in my note-book,—let me see—under the head "democratic drinks."—"Take your mint, fresh and unbruised, and put it in a clean tumbler; pour—" but no! I would rather not tell you, for who knows, if once you get the recipe you may be tempted to set to and make the liquor. And if once you taste it, you will probably make more;—when you are hot to cool you —when you are cold to warm you, and so forth. There must be a peculiar spell about it, for I have seen in America many men of talent, and good sense otherwise, with every reason consequent upon position in life to render them orderly, yet lower themselves and ruin their health by giving way to a vice, which more than any other breeds a loathsome equality between the man of worth and the worthless man. Who knows, that if you get hold of the recipe, instead of being an orderly, sober member of society, a loyal subject, and a good Tory; you will get muzzy, and hot-brained, and begin to fret about reform, and democratic forms of government,—doubt your Bible—despise your country—hate your King—fight cocks, and race like a Virginian,—swear profanely like a Western man— covet your neighbours' goods like a Yankee speculator —and end by turning Radical Reformer![13]

Latrobe's is the earliest description of the mint julep after it had come of age as a social drink and was to be had at American bars and taverns. Had he not played the tease about the receipt for it, he doubtless would have credit for introducing the mint julep to England. Instead, that bit of minor fame belongs to another English traveller later in the same decade, Captain Frederick Marryat.[14]

"Let it not be supposed," wrote Captain Marryat in describing New York City's preparations for celebrating the Fourth of July in 1837, "that there was any deficiency in the very necessary articles of potation on this auspicious day: no! the booths were loaded with porter, ale, cider, mead, brandy, wine, ginger-beer, pop, soda-water, whiskey, rum, punch, gin slings, cocktails, mint juleps, besides many other compounds, to name which nothing but the luxuriance of American-English could invent a word."[15]

Marryat was an acute observer of American life and wrote as engagingly of what he saw in his travels as he did in his score or more of popular novels. (He is now best remembered, perhaps, for *Mr. Midshipman Easy*, but his work is probably more familiar to a larger audience through Richard Wagner's opera *Die Fliegende Hollander*. It was adapted from Marryat's novel *The Phantom Ship*.) Living in hotels during his stay in the United States, Marryat was especially prepared as an expert on American drinking habits:

I always did consider that the English and the Swiss were the two nations who most indulged in potations; but on my arrival in the United States, I found that our descendants, in this point most assuredly, as they fain would be thought to do in all others, surpassed us altogether.

Impartiality compels me to acknowledge the truth: we must, in this instance, submit to a national defeat. There are many causes for this: first, the heat of the climate; then the changeableness of the climate; add to these, the cheapness of liquor in general, the early disfranchisement of the youth from all parental control, the temptation arising from the bar and association, and, lastly, the pleasantness, amenity, and variety of the potations. . . .

I have mentioned the principal causes to which must be assigned the propensity to drink, so universal in America. This is an undeniable fact. . . . It is not confined to the lower classes, but pervades the whole mass; of course, where there is most refinement, there is less intoxication, and in the southern and western states it is that the custom of drinking is most prevalent. . . .

The bar of an American hotel is generally a very large room on the basement, fitted up very much like our gin palaces in London, not so elegant in its decorations indeed, but on the same system. A long counter runs across it, behind which stand two or three barkeepers to wait upon the customers, and distribute the various potations, compounded from several rows of bottles behind them. Here the eye reposes on masses of pure crystal ice, large bunches of mint, decanters of every sort of wine, every variety of spirits, lemons, sugar, bitters, cigars and tobacco; it really makes one

11

feel thirsty, even going into a bar. Here you meet everybody and everybody meets you. . . .[16]

They say that the English cannot settle anything properly without a dinner. I am sure the Americans can fix nothing without a drink. If you meet, you drink; if you part, you drink; if you make acquaintance, you drink; if you close a bargain, you drink; they quarrel in their drink, and they make it up with a drink. They drink because it is hot; they drink because it is cold. If successful in elections, they drink and rejoice; if not, they drink and swear; they begin to drink early in the morning, they leave off late at night; they commence it early in life; and they continue it, until they soon drop into the grave. . . .

They say that you may always know the grave of a Virginian as, from the quantity of juleps he has drunk, mint invariably springs up where he has been buried.[17]

Captain Marryat's own fondness for a good drink—and his ability to hold more than one—undoubtedly stood him in good stead in his efforts to reach the Americans and to find out what they were thinking. "So much," he said,

has it become the habit to cement all friendship, and commence acquaintance by drinking, that it is a cause of serious offense to refuse, especially in a foreigner, as the Americans like to call the English. I was always willing to accommodate the Americans in this particular, as far as I could . . . ; that at times I drank much more than I wished is certain, yet still I gave most serious offense, especially in the west, because I would not drink early in the morning, or before dinner, which is a general custom in the states, although much more prevalent in the south and west, where it is literally: "Stranger, will you drink or fight?"[18]

He commented at length on the Americans' fondness for any and all types of drinks, on the phenomenal consumption of champagne, and the special popularity of Madeira. "But," he declared, "the Americans do not confine themselves to foreign wines or liquors; they have every variety at home, in the shape of compounds, such as mint-julep and its varieties; slings in all their varieties; cocktails."[19]

This travelling Englishman, like many another connoisseur of drinks, fell especially in love with the mint julep and, like nearly every one of its devotees, had his special way of making it. "I must . . . ," he noted,

descant a little upon the mint julep, as it is, with the thermometer at 100°, one of the most delightful and insinuating potations that ever was invented, and may be drunk with equal satisfaction when the thermometer is as low as 70°. There are many varieties, such as those composed of Claret, Madeira, etc.; but the ingredients of the real mint-julep are as follows. I learnt how to make them, and succeeded pretty well. Put into a tumbler about a dozen sprigs of the tender shoots of mint, upon them put a spoonful of white sugar, and equal proportions of peach and common brandy, so as to fill up one third, or perhaps a little less. Then take rasped or pounded ice, and fill up the tumbler. Epicures rub the lips of the tumbler with a piece of fresh pineapple, and the tumbler itself is very often encrusted outside with stalactites of ice. As the ice melts, you drink. I once overheard two ladies talking in the room next to me, and one of them said: "Well, if I have a weakness for any one thing, it is for a mint-julep"—a very amiable weakness, and proving her good sense and good taste. They are, in fact, like the American ladies, irresistible.[20]

The grandfather of bar guides is *How To Mix Drinks; or, The Bon-Vivant's Companion*, by Jerry Thomas, published in New York in 1862. Thomas called the julep a "peculiarly American beverage" and said that in the Southern states it "is more popular than any other."[21] He credited Marryat with popularizing it in England, quoted the traveller's receipt, and then gave his own:

Mint Julep
(Use large bar glass.)

1 table-spoonful of white pulverized sugar.
2½ do   water, mix well with a spoon.

Take three or four sprigs of fresh mint, and press them well in the sugar and water, until the flavor of the mint is extracted; add one and a half wine-glass of Cognac brandy, and fill the glass with fine shaved ice, then draw out the sprigs of mint and insert them in the ice with the stems downward, so that the leaves will be above, in the shape of a bouquet; arrange berries, and small pieces of sliced orange on top in a tasty manner, dash with Jamaica rum, and sprinkle white sugar on top. Place a straw as represented in the cut, and you have a julep that is fit for an emperor.[22]

Thomas added four more julep receipts—for a brandy julep, for a gin julep, for a whiskey julep, and for a pineapple julep.[23] The listing of the whiskey julep is important as the first recorded bartender's receipt of what has come to be the twentieth-century mint julep, though ingenious Kentuckians and Virginians thought out this version for themselves long before.

Theodore Irwin states:

The mint julep was introduced into England back in 1845 by William Heyward Trapier, a wealthy South Carolinian who brought along several casks of bourbon to sustain him on his trip. Visiting Oxford, he set up mint juleps for some students. Their delight so moved Mr. Trapier that he established an endowment in perpetuity to provide all Oxford students and their guests with free drinks each June 1. Mint Julep Day has been observed at Oxford ever since.[24]

A pretty story, but only partially true: William Trapier did visit Oxford, did introduce the mint julep to some of the undergraduates, and did leave an endowment to provide it—but only at New College. Marryat, however, had already introduced it in England, and the "several casks of bourbon" are pure assumption. In truth, William Heyward Trapier, a wealthy South Carolina rice planter, visited at New College in the spring of 1845. There he enjoyed the hospitality of the warden and fellows of one of the University's oldest colleges. When he was asked by the steward what he would like to drink, he requested a mint julep and was astounded to learn that it was unknown there. He proceeded to demonstrate how the drink should be made. It was an immediate—and great—success. Trapier had already charmed his hosts; his mint julep sealed his popularity. He left New College promising to return, but he never did, though an empty place is kept for him each June 1. On that night mint juleps are served at New College, Trapier is toasted as their donor, and the hospitality of the College is ready to welcome any descendant of his. Trapier's mint julep is Captain Marryat's version, a base of apricot brandy—but with bourbon added. The Trapier–New College receipt can be wheedled from the College's present steward; but, unless pressed, he fails to mention what he regards as the julep's "secret ingredient," the bourbon.[25]

In a charming decoration of history David Ogg, an emeritus fellow of New College, told the story of the Trapier–New College mint julep in the *South Carolina Historical Magazine* essentially as it is told at Oxford and confirming Trapier's gift of an endowment to provide the annual libations. Ogg adds:

For the purpose of the annual free round of mint julep, Trapier, with that gentlemanly exuberance so characteristic of the Old South Carolinian, caused a silver cup, of about 1740, to be engraved. The Latin inscription may well have been his own, but probably he was helped out by the Junior Fellows. The cup, a fine specimen of elaborately ornamented early Georgian silver, is about $5\frac{1}{2}$ inches high, and as "The Mint Julep Cup" has long been one of the most treasured pieces of plate in the College. Any South Carolinian who visits New College can see it by applying to the Steward of Junior Common Room. The inscription is as follows:

Coll.[egio] B.[eatae] V.[irginis] M.[ariae] Winton.[iensis] in Oxon.[ia]
D.[ono] D.[edit]
Gul.[ielmus] Heyward Trapier
Carolin.[iensis] Merid.[ionalis] America.[ensis]
In Usum Soc.[iorum] Jun.[iorum]
1845

The above may be translated thus: "Presented to the College of the Blessed Virgin Mary of Winchester in Oxford [the formal name of New College] for the use of the Junior Fellows by William Heyward Trapier of South Carolina in America 1845."[26]

As a visiting professor at the University of South Carolina in 1956–57, Mr. Ogg graciously returned Trapier's compliment to his college. He obtained a cup similar in size and design to New College's "Mint Julep Cup." Then, with the consent of New College and of the University of South Carolina, he caused this cup to be engraved on one side with the arms of the College and of the University, side by side; and on the other, with an inscription recording this happy association of 1845 and its renewal more than a century later by one who [had] many times seen that vacant place at table and never imagined that he would one day experience the friendliness and generosity of Trapier's homeland.[27]

The Old South reached its zenith in the decades just before the Civil War, at least in the rose-colored hindsight of the descendants of the Confederates. John Reuben Thompson, a Richmond editor, librarian, poet, and critic of some note, sent for reading at a banquet celebrating the anniversary of the Old Dominion Society of New York City, May 15, 1860, a rhymed toast that concludes with a description of the mint julep and names it as the drink of Virginia and of the nation:

> Then, brothers of the good old State,
>   Permit an absent rhymer
> To pledge the day you celebrate,
>   But not in Rudesheimer.
> He likes, whatever others think,
>   Virginia's own libation,
> A whiskey julep is the drink
>   That typifies the nation!
>
> The ice we take of liquid blue
>   From Wenham's crystal fountains,

The whiskey sparkles with the dew
　　Of old Virginia's mountains—
The sugar borrow without stint
　　From sunny Opelousas,
By every stream springs up the mint,
　　From Kennebec's to Coosa's:—

Que voulez-vous? 'Tis this—we wait
　　A wheat straw from the prairie.
(The Hoosier or the *Sucker* State,
　　Their practice does not vary,)
Here North and South and East and West
　　Are met in sweet communion—
Now drain this cup—this toast is best,
　　VIRGINIA AND THE UNION![28]

It was this period of *ante-bellum* confidence and plenty that was warmly sentimentalized more than a generation later by Clarence Ousley:

When the mint is in the liquor and its fragrance on the glass
It breathes a recollection that can never, never pass—
When the South was in the glory of a never-ending June
The strings were on the banjo and the fiddle was in tune,
And we reveled in the plenty that we thought could never pass
And lingered at the julep in the ever-brimming glass.[29]

War was to bring an end to all that. But reaction against intemperance was slowly changing the drinking habits of Americans. Dr. Waring had

19

called excessive drinking "the curse of our community" and "a fair object of legislative correction."[30] Massachusetts, trying to control the sale of alcoholic beverages, passed its unwise and ineffective "fifteen gallon law" in 1838.[31] Maine achieved the first state prohibition on whiskey in 1851, and Vermont, New Hampshire, Rhode Island, and Connecticut (where that early prohibition was never enforced) soon followed suit. Temperance societies abounded. The moral force of the Protestant churches was thrown against liquor.[32] Citizens still drank freely and fully, but drinking as a social art and practice was in disfavor by the time the Old South became the Confederacy. In few of the multitudinous reminiscences of the Confederates is it even mentioned, and the court cases and military records which testify to the widespread drunkenness refer generally to rot-gut whiskey and white-lightning, not to mint juleps.

Any diffidence there may have been about writing on drinking habits did not, of course, apply to the inevitable, seemingly ubiquitous, English traveller. Sir William Howard Russell, who made his reputation as a pioneer war correspondent during the Crimean War, came to America in 1861 as a special correspondent of the London *Times*. His forthright reporting managed to offend Confederates and Federals alike, for he was caustic in his comments on slavery while he was in the South and, later, in the North was vilified and, in legendary Chinese fashion, blamed for the Yankee defeat and given the soubriquet "Bull Run" Russell because of his full and damning account of the First Battle of Manassas.

Russell first mentioned the mint julep in his description of his voyage down Chesapeake Bay from Baltimore to Fortress Monroe. "On my way to the upper deck," he wrote,

I observed the bar was crowded by gentlemen engaged in consuming, or waiting for, cocktails or mint-juleps. The latter, however, could not be had just now in such perfection as usual, owing to the inferior condition of the mint. In the matter of drinks, how hospitable the Americans are! I was asked to take as many as would have rendered me incapable of drinking again; my excuse on the plea of inability to grapple with cocktails and the like before breakfast, was heard with surprise, and I was earnestly entreated to abandon so bad a habit.[33]

Russell was no temperance man. He was wined and dined by the elite and famous of the Confederacy as he toured towards New Orleans, but he did not detail his drinks or his dinners. He wrote, however, a passage about his sojourn in New Orleans that must have warmed the hearts of the temperance set. Russell visited the city jail with the sheriff and reported:

Speaking of the numerous crimes committed in New

Orleans, the sheriff declared it was a perfect hell on earth, and that nothing would ever put an end to murders, manslaughters, and deadly assaults till it was made penal to carry arms; but by law every American citizen may walk with an armoury round his waist if he likes. Bar-rooms, cocktails, mint-juleps, gambling houses, political discussions, and imperfect civilization do the rest.[34]

After visiting New Orleans, Russell returned to the North, viewed the battle at Manassas at first hand, and retired to Washington. There he again wrote of mint juleps—in a time-honored context:

July 27th.—So ill to-day from heat, bad smells in the house, and fatigue, that I sent for Dr. Miller, a great, fine Virginia practitioner, who ordered me powders to be taken in "mint juleps." Now mint juleps are made of whiskey, sugar, ice, very little water, and sprigs of fresh mint, to be sucked up after the manner of sherry cobbler, if it so be pleased, with a straw.

"A powder every two hours, with a mint julep. Why, that's six a day, Doctor. Won't that be rather intoxicating?"

"Well, sir, that depends on the constitution. You'll find they will do you no harm, even if the worst takes place."

Day after day, till the month was over and August had come, I passed in a state of powder and julep, which the Virginia doctor declared saved my life.[35]

The classic description of the mint julep properly served is part of the Confederate record. It is embedded in *Destruction and Reconstruction*, the personal narrative of General Richard Taylor, son of United States President Zachary Taylor and brother-in-law of Confederate States President Jefferson Davis. Douglas Southall Freeman described Taylor as "the one Confederate general who possessed literary art that approached the first rank."[36] There is no better evidence of that literary art than Taylor's account of a breakfast in Orange County while moving with "Stonewall" Jackson's troops from the Valley to the battlefields before Richmond in the late spring of 1862:

That night we camped between Charlottesville and Gordonsville, in Orange County, the birthplace of my father. A distant kinsman, whom I had never met, came to invite me to his house in the neighborhood. Learning that I always slept in camp, he seemed so much distressed as to get my consent to breakfast with him, if he would engage to have breakfast at the barbarous hour of sunrise. His house was a little distant from the road; so, the following morning, he sent a mounted groom to show me the way. My aide, young [James] Hamilton, accompanied me, and Tom [Taylor's groom] of course followed. It was a fine old mansion, surrounded by well-kept grounds. This immediate region had not yet been touched by war. Flowering plants and rose trees, in full bloom, attested to the glorious wealth of June. On the broad portico, to welcome us, stood the host, with his fresh, charming wife, and, a little retired, a white-headed butler. Greetings over with host and lady, this delightful creature, with ebon face beaming hospitality, advanced holding a salver, on which rested a huge silver goblet filled with Virginia's nectar, mint julep. Quantities of cracked ice rattled refreshingly in the goblet; sprigs of fragrant mint peered above its broad rim; a mass of white sugar, too sweetly indolent to melt, rested on the mint; and, like rose buds on a snow bank, luscious strawberries crowned the sugar. Ah! that julep. Mars ne'er received such tipple from the hands of Ganymede. Breakfast was announced, and what a breakfast! A beautiful service, snowy table cloth, damask napkins, long unknown; above all, a lovely woman in crisp gown, with more and handsomer roses on her cheek than in her garden. 'Twas an idyl in the midst of the stern realities of war! The table groaned beneath its viands. Sable servitors brought in, hot and hot from the kitchen, cakes of wondrous forms, inventions of the tropical imagination of Africa, inflamed by Virginia hospitality. I was a rather moderate trencherman, but the performance of Hamilton was Gargantuan, alarming. Duty dragged us from this Eden; yet in hurried adieus I did not forget to claim of the fair hostess the privilege of a cousin. I watched Hamilton narrowly for a time. The youth wore a sodden, apoplectic look, quite out of his usual brisk form. A gallop of some miles put him right, but for many days he dilated on the breakfast with the gusto of one of Hannibal's veterans on the delights of Capua.[37]

John Esten Cooke, Jeb Stuart's adjutant and ordnance officer and the novelist most intimately connected with the Army of Northern Virginia—both in its activities and in recording the spirit of that incomparable army in his novels—relates in a highly autobiographical novel the occasion of an equally bountiful feast, a dinner in Stuart's camp for which the delicacies were provided from a captured Federal wagon. Stuart was a teetotaller, but the others of his staff were not; there were mint juleps for this party too:

[Captain] Bogy . . . disappeared in the direction of the wagon.

What does Bogy return with? Is it not a brace of bottles? It is a brace of bottles, with rich labels and green seals. Bogy sets them on the table—all eyes admire!

His aid ["a dilapidated African staff officer," he had previously been termed] brings him mint and ice from the spring—a glass dish of white sugar from the wonderful wagon; and then behold! a long row of rich cut-glass goblets! The guests cease to wonder farther; they gaze in silence at the great magician. . . .

Bogy draws a cork—a rich bouquet of Otard brandy, old and mellow, is inhaled. Some young officers who have just joined the company look faint. The odor overcomes their sensitive nerves. Old Otard on the outpost!

With the hand of a master, Bogy mixes his liquids, and behold, a long row of goblets full of julep, from whose Alpine heights of ice springs the fragrant mint! As the contents of those bright goblets disappear down the throats of the guests, their eyes close, and Bogy towers before them, the greatest of mortals.[38]

A younger and less successful Confederate novelist was Clifford Anderson Lanier, brother of the poet Sidney Lanier. His novel *Thorn-Fruit* is full of the wartime adventures of the two brothers. It is in a large part laid in the tidewater area of Southside Virginia and does not fail in singing the praises of the mint juleps of the region. Lanier refers to the julep once as a pre-breakfast drink, once as a stirrup-cup, and once—on a hot June afternoon—as "a vial from the moon" to bring back the wits.[39]

Another Confederate, General William B. Taliaferro of Gloucester County, Virginia, had, in a youthful essay at poetry, published long before the War, lauded the mint julep in rhymes less poetic (so unpoetic, in fact, that, for the most part, they will not bear quotation) than Taylor's prose. Its introductory note and introductory verses, however, comprise an interesting confirmation of the mint julep as a pre-breakfast potation:

It is jocularly said of the lower Virginians that they never rise from their beds in the morning, until they are persuaded to do so by the notes of the Mockingbird, whose favorite note most nearly resembles the words, julap, julap, julap, quickly repeated.

This anecdote suggested the following lines.

The Mocking-bird sat on the topmost spray
Of the tree where he's whiled the night away:
Morning broke 'round him, yet never did he,
Brave old bird, cease to carrol his glee.
Julap, julap, julap, quoth he,

As he chanted his song on the leafless tree.
I prithee awake from thy slumbers to greet
The glass of gay julap, julap so sweet.[40]

A poem of considerably more merit is Mrs. Fanny Murdaugh Downing's *Pluto: Being the Sad Story and Lamentable Fate of the Fair Minthe*, published at Raleigh, North Carolina, in 1867. In *Pluto* the elderly and "very married" god falls in love with Minthe, daughter of the river Cocytus, but loses her when the jealous Proserpina turns her into an herb. To restore him from melancholy Venus decides:

> ". . . since Pluto can't lose sight
> Of *Minthe*'s memory, and despite
> Her loss still loves her, it is right
> His love should yield him vast delight,
> And not his peace and pleasure blight.
> You're conscious," here she curtsied low,
> "The strongest passions Gods can know,
> Are love and liquor; I'll combine
> The two, and make a drink divine,
> And when you taste it, I opine,
> You'll think it Nectar's self outshine!"[41]

In the next section of the poem the concoction of Venus's mint julep is detailed:

> The Goddess from her bosom took
>   The fragrant herb still freshly dripping
> With crystal dew-drops from the brook.
>   And with her pearly fingers nipping

Its tender leaves, bade it extol
Sweet *Minthe*'s charms without control,
And with ecstatic rapture roll
Sublimed by Love, through Pluto's soul;
She then, within a gilded bowl,
   The fragrant leaflets lavish heaping
That their aroma tinge the whole,
   Passed it along to Neptune's keeping.
He kept the bowl just long enough
   To make it cold; then with a mighty
Improper oath said: "Blast the stuff—
   I'm going back to Amphitrite,
So farewell mates, till next I see ye!"
   Bright ivey-covered Bacchus bore
A mighty flask of liquor glorious
   To make the hearts of mortals soar
O'er earth, up to a height uproarious!
   Then as he poured, he charged the vine,
That its most subtle powers combine,
   And with mysterious art entwine
To form with *Minthe*, a sublime
Ethereal essence, all divine!
Apollo said, the only thing
   That he could see the drink required
Which would a heightened pleasure bring,
   Or make it more to be desired—
To raise it to the highest stand,
   Was more of mind commixed with matter,
And so he would with skillful hand,
   An intellectual influence scatter,
And charge imaginations's gift,
The drinker's mind, on pinions swift,
Past heaven's golden gates to lift.

Mars, who still close by Venus stood,
  That he might be excused, requested;
He thought the liquid all too good
  To be with warlike powers invested!
But still he would an influence add
  Which might impart a higher flavor,
So it, unless the drinker had
  Imbibed too much, should make him braver!
Said Mercury, "Don't let it slip
Beyond our reach, before we dip
Some sweetness in; let Venus sip
And yield it honey from her lip!"
The Goddess filled a crystal cup
And to her rosy lip put up
The sparkling mixture; at its taste
She left her seat with eager haste,
And gliding quick to Pluto's side
The goblet to his mouth applied.
Then cried, with clear exultant voice:
"Oh! *Pluto*, over Fate rejoice!
Drink perfect solace to thy pain,
And find thy *Minthe* live again!"[42]

Clearly the mint julep originated in the northern
Virginia tidewater, spread soon to Maryland,[43] and
eventually all along the seaboard and even to trans-
montane Kentucky. It was first made with local
whiskey (which would have been rye) and was
refined by the 1830's to the receipt of Marryat.
While the julep of *ante-bellum* Virginia undoubtedly was usually mixed with brandy as its base, the
whiskey julep continued as the drink of the less

sophisticated elements of society; the necessary ingredients were readily at hand: home-distilled whiskey and home-grown mint.

After the Civil War, when home-grown ingredients were all most Southerners could afford, the bourbon mint julep gradually became the standard, and most Southerners today are surprised to learn that their regional drink was ever, or can be now, made with any other liquor. The marriage of bourbon and mint does indeed form, to use Mrs. Downing's words, "a sublime ethereal essence, all divine."

In the post-prohibition era of the twentieth century bourbon has established itself as the national beverage of America almost as clearly as Scotch whiskey is the national drink of England. Such was not always the case. The first American commercial distilleries, in the seventeenth century, were in New England, where rum was distilled from molasses imported from the West Indies. Rum was the drink of the common people and remained so until the latter half of the eighteenth century when rye whiskey distilled in Pennsylvania, Maryland, and northern Virginia became as popular. As the Scotch-Irish immigrants moved westward they took their copper stills with them and, in western Pennsylvania, found that corn grew better than rye and distilled equally well. They also discovered that more money was to be made by distilling whiskey from the corn and shipping it east in barrels than by the more cumbersome shipment of whole grain.

Whiskey made from a corn mash is said to have been distilled at Jamestown as early as 1622, but rye became the standard whiskey of the Tidewater during Colonial and early Federal times.[44] Evan Williams owned the first distillery in Kentucky, at Louisville in 1783. The Reverend Elijah Craig is often cited as the originator of bourbon whiskey. He was distilling corn at Georgetown in Scott County in 1789.[45] In the same year Daniel Stewart advertised a still for sale in Lexington and may have produced a sour-mash whiskey there.[46] Jacob Beam, progenitor of a family which still makes fine Kentucky bourbon, was, relatively, a Jacob-come-lately, moving out from Virginia to Clermont, Kentucky, in 1795.[47]

Henry G. Crowgey, author of the definitive history of bourbon in its early years, dismisses the possibility of tying the origin of bourbon to any single distiller, place, or date. He notes that the Kentucky whiskey produced in the pre–Civil War years "could not possibly have met modern specifications for bourbon whiskey." He says:

Herein lies the principal difficulty in considering most of the various aspects of early Kentucky distilling—in particular, the first bourbon whiskey. The writers and historians of the late nineteenth century yielded to the

31

temptation of applying their own standards to the distilling practices of the late eighteenth century. Needless to say, these errors have been perpetuated and compounded by the writing profession of a later day.

Crowgey demonstrates that the first printed use of the term "bourbon whiskey" appeared in a Bourbon County newspaper (the Maysville *Western Citizen*) in 1821 and that the use of the term did not become statewide until "by 1840." By the 1850's "Old Bourbon" had found its way generally into the American language.[48]

In its initial state, straight from the still, bourbon is colorless. What Irvin S. Cobb called "red likker" comes later, after infusion with some rye whiskey and proper aging. The corn is brewed for the still with barley malt, hence the name "John Barleycorn." The color itself comes during the aging process, from the charred oaken barrels. Whatever arguments there be concerning its origin or its uses, there is general agreement that the limestone-based water of Kentucky produces a whiskey of unusual sweetness and lightness.

Kentuckians have ever been trying to make up for not being born Virginians. They have seized on their special claim to bourbon whiskey as giving them the right also to arrogate the mint julep to themselves. Lawrence S. Thompson, Kentucky gentleman, librarian and classicist, and historian of considerable ability, becomes an arrant fabricator where the julep is concerned:

Pretenders and upstarts in Maryland, Georgia, and even remote Louisiana have alleged that the mint julep was invented in their native habitats. Knavish Georgians have attempted to produce "the very dream of drinks" from corn whiskey sweetened with molasses. One Bluegrasser has reported that barbarous New Yorkers will gulp down juleps hideously concocted with creme de menthe and maraschino cherries. There is but one bona fide mint julep, and it is as indigenous to the Bluegrass as gin and bitters is to the diet of a London charwoman.[49]

Thompson asserts: "None of the pretenders to the honor of inventing the julep has ever produced a recipe as convincing as the marvelous formula of Judge Soule Smith, famed Lexington attorney and wit who flourished in the late nineteenth century."[50]

Here is Judge Smith's receipt:

But in the Blue Grass land there is a softer sentiment —a gentler soul. There where the wind makes waves of the wheat and scents itself with the aroma of new-mown hay, there is no contest with the world outside. On summer days when, from his throne, the great sun dictates his commands, one may look forth across broad acres where the long grass falls and rises as the winds may blow it. He can see the billowy slopes far off, each heaving as the zephyrs touch it with caressing hand. Sigh of the earth with never a sob, the wind comes to the Blue Grass. A sweet sigh, a loving one; a tender sigh, a lover's touch, she gives the favored land. And the moon smiles at her caressing and the sun gives benediction to the lovers. Nature and earth are one—married by the wind and sun and whispering leaflets on the happy tree.

Then comes the zenith of man's pleasure. Then comes the julep—the mint julep. Who has not tasted one has lived in vain. The honey of Hymettus brought no such solace to the soul; the nectar of the Gods is tame beside it. It is the very dream of drinks, the vision of sweet quaffings. The Bourbon and the mint are lovers. In the same land they live, on the same food are fostered. The mint dips its infant leaf into the same stream that makes the Bourbon what it is. The corn grows in the level lands through which small streams meander. By the brookside the mint grows. As the little wavelets pass, they glide up to kiss the feet of the growing mint, the mint bends to salute them. Gracious and kind it is, living only for the sake of others. The crushing of it only makes its sweetness more apparent. Like a woman's heart, it gives its sweetest aroma when bruised. Among the first to greet the spring, it comes. Beside the gurgling brooks that make music in the pastures it lives and thrives. When the Blue Grass begins to shoot its gentle sprays toward the sun, mint comes, and its sweetest soul drinks at the crystal brook. It is virgin then. But soon it must be married to Old Bourbon. His great heart, his warmth of temperament, and that affinity which no one understands, demands the wedding. How shall it be? Take from the cold spring some water, pure as angels are; mix with it sugar until it seems like oil. Then take a glass and

34

crush your mint within it with a spoon—crush it around the borders of the glass and leave no place untouched. Then throw the mint away—it is a sacrifice. Fill with cracked ice the glass; pour in the quantity of Bourbon which you want. It trickles slowly through the ice. Let it have time to cool, then pour your sugared water over it. No spoon is needed, no stirring is allowed—just let it stand a moment. Then around the brim place sprigs of mint, so that the one who drinks may find a taste and odor at one draught.

When it is made, sip it slowly. August suns are shining, the breath of the south wind is upon you. It is fragrant, cold and sweet—it is seductive. No maiden's kiss is tenderer or more refreshing; no maiden's touch could be more passionate. Sip it and dream—you cannot dream amiss. Sip it and dream, it is a dream itself. No other land can give so sweet a solace for your cares; no other liquor soothes you so in melancholy days. Sip it and say there is no solace for the soul, no tonic for the body like Old Bourbon whiskey.[51]

A fine tribute, indeed. It is perhaps the ultimate accolade to the mint julep, but it is no evidence at all as to who invented the mint julep. Thompson, a former FBI man, should know better. He produces no substantive evidence on the origins of the julep, but rests his case on rhetoric. Gerald Carson says with authority, but without citing any, that Kentuckians "were awarding silver julep cups as prizes at county fairs as long ago as 1816" but then weakens his case by citing Thompson as an authority on the mint julep and quoting from his "pretenders and usurpers" paragraph.[52]

Undoubtedly apocryphal, but in the lack of any firmer record of how the mint julep came to Kentucky, a story worth retelling is the anecdote headed "Not an Uncommon Case" from the Confederates' *Southern Punch*:

A traveler from Virginia, as his appearance indicated, stopped at a comfortable wayside inn, in Kentucky, one night years ago. The landlord was a jovial, whole souled fellow, as landlords were in those days, and gave the stranger the best entertainment his table and bar could afford, as well as his own merry company to make him glad.

Early in the morning the stranger was up and looking around, when he espied a rich bed of mint in the garden. He straightway sought Boniface, and indignant at what he supposed his inhospitality, in setting plain whiskey before him when the means of brewing nectar was so easy of access, he dragged him forth to the spot, and pointing with his finger at the mint, he exclaimed:

"I say, landlord, will you be good enough to say what this is?"

"A bed of mint," said the somewhat astonished landlord.

"And will you please tell me what it is used for?"

"Well, don't exactly know, 'cept the old woman dries it sometimes with the other yarbs."

The Virginian almost turned pale at the enormity of the assertion.

"And do you mean to tell me that you do not know what a mint julep is?"

"Not 'cept it is something like sage tea, stranger."

"Sage tea! Go right along to the house, get a bucket of ice, loaf sugar, and your best liquor."

The landlord obeyed, and the stranger soon made his appearance with a handful of fragrant, dewy mint, and then they brewed and drank, and drank again; breakfast was over, and the stranger's horse was brought out, only to be ordered back.

Through the livelong day they brewed and drank, one or two neighbors dropping in, who were par-takers, and late in the night their orgies kept up; ere they made it bed time, the landlord and the Virginia guest, who had initiated him into the pleasure of mint julep, were sworn brothers, and when the latter de-parted next morning, Boniface exacted the pledge that he would stop on his return, and stay as long as he pleased, free of cost.

The stranger's business, however, detained him longer than he expected, and it was the next summer before he came back.

Riding up late in the evening, he gave his horse to an old negro who was at the gate, and at the same time inquired:

"Well, Sam, how is your master?"

"Yonder he comes," said the negro, pointing to a youth who was approaching.

"I mean your old master, too!"

"Old massa! him done dead dis three months."

"Dead! What was the matter with him? He was in fine health when I left him."

"Yes, you see, massa stranger, one of dem Virginny

37

genman come 'long here las' year, and show'd him *how to eat grass in his liquor*; he like it so well he done stuck to it 'till it kill him," said the darkey, shaking his head.[53]

However the mint julep was introduced to Kentucky, it found a true home there. It is part and parcel of Kentucky lore and of Kentucky social life and hospitality. Mass-produced juleps are hawked at the Kentucky Derby. Members of the Gen'l P. G. T. Beauregard Marching and Burial Society celebrate May 28 (the general's birthdate) as the opening of the julep season.[54] Juleps supposed to be the best in the world are served at Louisville's Pendennis Club.

Ranking with the julep of the Pendennis Club and equally fine, each in its own way, are the mint juleps served in the Williamsburg Inn, Richmond's Commonwealth Club, the Greenbrier at White Sulphur Springs, Atlanta's Piedmont Driving Club, and Savannah's venerable Oglethorpe Club (where, however, the drinker must bring his own mint). The standard modern receipt is no better stated than in the delightful *The Williamsburg Art of Cookery* of Mrs. Helen Bullock:

To make a true Mint Julep

There is only one approved and authentic Method of making a *Virginia* Mint Julep—and to this Truth every good *Virginian* will agree. After many Years of Study and patient Investigation the Author is able to report that on this precise Method, few Virginians are able to agree. A Symposium held with some of the better Julep-makers finds them in Agreement with the following:

A Julep Glass or Goblet is not the proper Container in which to serve Salads composed of Oranges, Pineapples, Lemons, Cherries and other outlandish Fruits, such as are commonly found in some Establishments which pretend to serve Juleps.

Two Things will inevitably ruin any Julep, the first of which is too much Sugar, and the second too little Whisky. Having observed carefully the foregoing, take a long, thin, glass Tumbler or a Silver Goblet and place it on a Tray. In the Bottom place the Leaves from a Sprig of Mint and add one half Tablespoonful of powdered Sugar. Crush the Mint well with the Sugar, and dissolve in a Tablespoonful of Water. Pack the Glass full with very finely-crushed Ice, trying not to wet the Outside of the Glass. Pour into this a Glass of Whisky (Whisky distilled from Corn is traditional but that made from Rye or other Grain is permissible). Some Authorities, having packed the Glass well with Ice, pour in the Whisky until the Glass is full. Stir gently until the Glass is well-frosted on the Outside. Decorate on Top with three Sprigs of Mint and serve.[55]

Harriet Ross Colquitt gave a twentieth-century julep receipt a bit closer to the versions of the early nineteenth century in *The Savannah Cook Book*. This version may be rightfully considered the ancient mint julep of Georgians:

Put a teaspoon of sugar in a tall glass or silver goblet.

Add just sufficient water to dissolve sugar.

Break off tender leaves of mint and add to the syrup.

Crush mint leaves vigorously with a small wooden pestle.

Allow a jigger and a half of rye whiskey to each glass and stir well.

Fill glass full of finely crushed ice and stir again.

Add more ice and agitate gently.

Put slices of apple and orange and pineapple around the sides of glass, and strawberries and cherries on top, and lastly, sprigs of slightly bruised mint.

Sprinkle a little sugar on top . . . and sip![56]

Controversy surrounding the mint julep does not end with a determination of its origins. Most julep drinkers will concede that the true Kentucky mint julep, the julep of post-prohibition fame and popularity, is made with bourbon and are willing to drink toasts to the state

> Where the corn is full of kernels
> And the colonels full of corn.[57]

There are, however, vigorous proponents of minority viewpoints. In New Orleans a version of the julep is still made of brandy, with a bounty of fruit thrown in, and it may thus be had at the Boston Club (named for a card game, not for the Yankee city).[58] The mint-julep receipt of Manila's Bay View Hotel, famed in the years before World War II, calls for a jigger of bourbon or rye, a pony of bacardi oro, and two dashes of Spanish brandy.[59]

Another veteran receipt demands a wine glass of bourbon with a barspoon of Jamaica rum on top.[60] Marylanders will insist that their mint juleps be made of rye. (Irvin S. Cobb said of his friend H. L. Mencken, the sage of Baltimore in the first half of this century and an expert on drinks alcoholic: "Any guy who'd put rye in a mint julep and crush the leaves, would put scorpions in a baby's bed.")[61]

Gourmet magazine published an article, "Of Myths and Mint," in June 1963 in which it gave the directions for "Gourmet's Mint Julep":

In a silver mug or chilled glass put 3 or 4 fresh mint leaves and 1 teaspoon each of sugar and water. Bruise the mint leaves gently with a wooden muddler and stir the mixture until the sugar is dissolved. Pack the mug to the brim with finely crushed ice. Pour in 1 jigger bourbon and stir briskly until a frost appears on the outside of the container. Fill it to the brim with bourbon. Dust a sprig of mint with confectioners' sugar, cut the stem short, and set the mint in the ice to garnish the drink.[62]

This article brought into flame all the mint-julep controversies, kindled in *Gourmet* a month earlier by a letter from a reader in Nebraska giving the receipt for a "Yankee Mint Julep." The directions in that receipt are almost word-for-word those in the receipt General Buckner wrote out—until the essential ingredient is mentioned. Here, instead of Kentucky bourbon, the Nebraskan calls for one ounce of peach or apricot brandy and two ounces of Cognac and requires that one ounce of heavy, dark rum be poured on top.[63]

A reader of *Gourmet* in California quoted later editions of Jerry Thomas's *The Bartender's Guide* for "The Real Georgia Mint Julep," made with peach brandy and cognac, the mint not crushed, but the whole drink stirred. A Tennesseean waxed long and strong on the necessity of using only 100 proof bourbon. A New Yorker (probably a displaced Southerner) also preferred 100 proof bourbon and insisted on "dark green mint leaves . . . bruised in the bottom of the goblet with one teaspoon of honey from the Tennessee mountains." She directed: "Never stir, circulate or disturb the contents. A julep needs tranquility and gentle handling."[64]

In 1968 *Gourmet* summed it up in an article, "Summer Drinks," saying:

The julep conjures up visions of pleasant, soporific afternoons on ante-bellum plantations, but the controversies surrounding it are as blazing as the Southern sun it tempers. Should the mint be mashed or bruised, plain or sugar-coated? Should it be presented as a single leaf or in glorious profusion? Is the addition of a little rum or liqueur to the bourbon mixture *de rigueur* or is it sacrilege—indeed, is bourbon itself a necessity?

The magazine then presented five more mint-julep receipts—with bourbon, cognac, *creme de menthe*, rum, and rye.[65]

The business of whether to crush or not to crush is, after the point of what kind of liquor, the largest point of controversy. All that is left to posterity of Latrobe's Tallahassee receipt is that the mint be "fresh and unbruised." The receipt for the Pendennis Club's potation requires that the mint not be crushed. Obviously, from Cobb's remark, Marylanders do crush the fragrant leaves. Most makers of the drink help free the flavor of the mint by at least bruising them gently.[66]

In a charmingly Southern story in *Sixes and Sevens* called "The Duplicity of Hargraves" O. Henry told the story of a dialect comedian who lived in Washington in the same boarding house as "Major Pendleton Talbot, of Mobile, sir, and his daughter, Miss Lydia Talbot." The actor and the impoverished but proud major became friends, and: "Sometimes, at night, when the young man would be coming upstairs to his room . . . , the major would appear at the door of his study and beckon archly to him. Going in, Hargraves would find a little table set with a decanter, sugar bowl, fruit, and a big bunch of fresh green mint." The major would then offer the young actor what he called " 'tired Nature's sweet restorer,'—one of our Southern juleps." The story continues:

43

It was a fascination to Hargraves to watch him make it. He took rank among the artists when he began, and he never varied the process. With what delicacy he bruised the mint; with what exquisite nicety he estimated the ingredients; with what solicitous care he capped the compound with the scarlet fruit glowing against the dark green fringe! And then the hospitality with which he offered it, after the selected oat straws had been plunged into its tinkling depths!

After some months the major learned of a new war drama to be produced in Washington, "The Magnolia Flower," and was told "that the South has very fair treatment in this play." He splurged on tickets for himself and Miss Lydia. Hargraves appeared in the play as "Col. Webster Calhoun." The major and his daughter watched the performance indignant and bewitched as they learned what a perfect study the young actor had made of his elderly friend, as they "saw the counterfeit presentment of a haughty Talbot 'dragged,' as the major afterward expressed it, 'through the slanderous mire of a corrupt stage.' " For, O. Henry says, "Colonel Calhoun was made up as nearly resembling Major Talbot as one pea does another. . . . Mr. Hargraves had used his opportunities well. He had caught the major's little idiosyncracies of speech, accent, and intonation and his pompous courtliness to perfection—exaggerating all to the purpose of the stage."

44

Hargraves's performance reached its height in the making of a mint julep in just the way Major Talbot had made them for him. The major's "delicate but showy science was reproduced to a hair's breadth—from his dainty handling of the fragrant weed—'the one-thousandth part of a grain too much pressure, gentlemen, and you extract the bitterness, instead of the aroma, of this heaven-bestowed plant'—to his solicitous selection of the oaten straws."[67]

This Hargraves-Talbot, or Talbot-Hargraves, statement can stand as the ultimate dictum on the crush-or-not-to-crush controversy. Perhaps the last word on the whole business of the mint julep should be the receipt of "Marse Henry" Watterson, the famous Louisville editor of two generations ago:

Pluck the mint gently from its bed, just as the dew of the evening is about to form upon it. Select the choicer sprigs only, but do not rinse them. Prepare the simple syrup and measure out a half-tumbler of whiskey. Pour the whiskey into a well-frosted silver cup, throw the other ingredients away and drink the whiskey.[68]

NOTES

1. A typescript of General Buckner's receipt was given to the author a number of years ago by the late Mrs. Nina Taliaferro Sanders (Mrs. H. O. Sanders) of "Warrington," Gloucester County, Va. Mrs. Sanders, who was the daughter of Confederate Gen. William B. Taliaferro, noted that the receipt had been sent to her by a gentleman of Boston who had been a recent guest at Warrington and had declared the juleps there "as good as the receipt."
2. Theodore Irwin, "About: Bourbon," *The New York Times Magazine*, March 8, 1964, p. 76.
3. John Milton, *Comus*, ll. 671–673.
4. *The American Museum*, I (1787), 215.
5. John Davis, *Travels of Four Years and a Half in the United States of America: During 1798, 1799, 1800, 1801 and 1802* (London: T. Ostell [etc.]; New-York, for R. Edwards, printer, Bristol, 1803).
6. Davis, *Travels of Four Years and a Half in the United States of America in 1798, 1799, 1800, 1801, and 1802 . . .* , with an introduction and notes by A. J. Morrison (New York: Henry Holt and Company, 1909), pp. 413–414.
7. *Ibid.*, p. 414.

Charles William Janson wrote similarly of a "sling": "The first craving of an American in the morning is for ardent spirits, mixed with sugar, mint, or some other hot herb, and which are called slings." *The Stranger in America* (London: J. Cundee, 1807), p. 299.

Arthur Singleton [*i.e.*, Henry Cogswell Knight] noted in 1816: "The first thing in the morning with many [Virginians], is the silver goblet of mint julep." *Letters from the South and West* (Boston: Richardson & Lord, 1824), p. 71.

In his delightful, hyperbolic spoof of the accounts of America by English travellers, James Kirke Paulding has his fictitious traveller note the propensity of Americans for snoring. "I was troubled to account for this habit," he declared, "until Dr. Thornton afterwards assured me they slept with their mouths wide open for the convenience of swallowing a mint julep, which was always poured down their throats before they awoke in the morning, to keep them from getting the intermittent fever." *John Bull in America; or, The New Munchausen* (London: John Miller, 1825), pp. 203–204.

8. [Marion Alexander Boggs, editor,] *The Alexander Letters, 1787–1900* (Savannah, Ga.: Privately printed for George C. Baldwin, 1910), pp. 16–17.

9. Gerald Carson, *Rum and Reform in Old New England* (Sturbridge, Mass.: Old Sturbridge Village [c.1966]), p. 10.

  A contemporaneous view of drinking and drunkenness, with a multitude of examples (drawn mostly from the southeastern states), is Mason Locke Weems's *The Drunkard's Looking Glass . . .* ([Philadelphia?] 1813). This rare tract was first published in 1812 as *God's Revenge Against Drunkenness*, but no copy of its first edition can now be located. Its lively, sensationalized text is available in Weems's *Three Discourses* (New York: Random House, 1929), pp. 49–136. Weems does not mention mint juleps as such, but he quotes the tavern bill of a "Col. A—— B——" on April 1, 1812, which includes at twenty-five cents each "3 Mint-slings before breakfast." P. 112.

10. MS which belonged to the late J. Fred Waring, Esq., of Savannah. (A typescript of this speech is in the collections of the Georgia Historical Society, Savannah.)

11. Charles Joseph Latrobe, *The Rambler in North America: MDCCCXXXII.–MDCCCXXXIII.*, 2d ed. (London: R. B. Seeley and W. Burnside, 1836), II, 58–60.

12. *Ibid.*, II, 60–61. A "hail-stone" (alternately "hail-storm") is insufficiently and incorrectly defined in Mitford M. Mathews's *A Dictionary of Americanisms on Historical Principles* (Chicago, Ill.: The University of Chicago Press [1956, c.1951]), p. 763. Mathews gives "hail-stone" merely as "some kind of drink" and under "hail-storm" quotes this passage from Latrobe, noting the word as a synonym for "mint julep." Latrobe would hardly have used it in the sequence in his sentence were that so. Correctly, a hail-stone or hail-storm was simply whiskey served with chunks of ice in it. It is so noted in Richard H. Thornton, *An American Glossary* (New York: Frederick Ungar Publishing Co. [1962]), I, 408. The word may be obsolete, as indicated by Mathews; the drink is not.

In his story "Putting a Black-Leg on Shore," Benjamin Drake told of "A numerous and peculiar race of *modern* gentlemen [who] may be found in the valley of the Mississippi." "They," Drake wrote, "are supposed to entertain an especial abhorrence of the prevailing *temperance* fanaticism; and, as a matter of conscience, enter a daily protest against it, by sipping 'mint-julaps' before breakfast, 'hail-storms' at dinner, and 'old Monongahela' at night." *Tales and Sketches from the Queen City* (Cincinnati: E. Morgan and Co., 1838), p. 27.

The author can find no explanation of the drink called "snow-storm." It seems logical, at least, to suppose that it was whiskey poured into a glass of rasped ice.

13. Latrobe, II, 61–62.
14. Likewise missing the chance to describe the mint julep and all its charms to English readers was Basil Hall, who, in his *Travels in America*, 3d. ed. (Edinburgh: Robert Cadell; London: Simpkin and Marshall, 1830), III, 71, notes in his account of his trip between Fredericksburg and Richmond in 1827: "Two of the gentlemen, our fellow passengers, were Virginian planters, very intelligent persons. . . . We stopped at ten different houses during the seventeen weary hours which it cost us to make out the 66 miles, and at each of these places our two friends got out, as they told us, to take a glass of mint julap—which I learnt from them was a species of dram."

Another English traveller who could have given a description earlier than Marryat's was the Rev. Andrew Reed. Reed saw his first mint julep in Louisville in 1834. He wrote: "On arriving at my hotel, I found its master, who is a colonel as well as tavern-keeper, busily engaged in making and distributing his mint-julep. It is a favorite mixture of spirits, mint, sugar, and water, and he has a high character for the just incorporation of the ingredients." Later, writing of the inn at Owensville, Ky., Reed mentioned that "here, as everywhere, mint-julep was the favourite draught." The Reverend Reed, who wrote the reports from the South while his co-author remained in the East, can probably be excused for not going into further detail about the julep as he was a strong temperance man and did not partake of one himself. Andrew Reed, *A Narrative of the Visit to the American Churches, by the Deputation from the Congregational Union of England and Wales*, by Andrew Reed and James Matheson (New York: Harper & Brothers, 1835), I, 122, 134.

15. Frederick Marryat, *A Diary in America, with Remarks on Its Institutions . . .* , ed., with notes and an introduction, by Sydney Jackman (New York: Alfred A. Knopf, 1962), p. 59.

Charles Dickens confirmed the rich vocabulary for describing American potations in his *American Notes* (1842). He wrote of the bar of his hotel in Boston: "There . . . the stranger is initiated into the mysteries of Gin-sling, Cocktail, Sangaree, Mint Julep, Sherry Cobbler, Timber Doodle, and other rare drinks." *American Notes and Pictures from Italy* (London [etc.]: Oxford University Press [1966]), p. 60. The language of tippling was equally extensive and robust. Weems wrote of what he designated as the first stage of drunkenness, "the FROLICKSOME or FOOLISH" stage: "At this stage of the disease, the patient goes by a variety of nick-names, all of them well befitting the contemptibleness of his character, such as BOOZY —GROGGY—BLUE—DAMP—TIPSY—FUDDLED—HAILY GAILY— HOW CAME YOU SO—HALF SHAVED—SWIPY—HAS GOT A DROP IN HIS EYE—HAS GOT HIS WET SHEET ABROAD—CUT IN THE CRAW—HIGH UP TO PICKING COTTON (Georgia)." P. 60.

16. This is obviously a description of a bar typical of a hotel in one of the principal cities. Of travel in rural areas Marryat, p. 377, wrote: "Of course, where the population and traffic are great, and the travelers who pass through numerous, the hotels are large and good; where, on the contrary, the road is less and less frequented, so do they decrease in importance, size, and respectability, until you arrive at the farm-house entertainment of Virginia and Kentucky; the grocery, or mere grog-shop, or the log house of the far west. The wayside inns are remarkable for their uniformity; the furniture of the bar-room is invariably the same: a wooden clock, map of the United States, map of the state, the Declaration of Independence, a looking-glass, with a hair-brush and comb hanging to it by strings, *pro bono publico*; sometimes with the extra embellishment of one or two miserable pictures, such as General Jackson scrambling upon a horse, with fire and steam coming out of his nostrils, going to the battle of New Orleans, etc., etc."

17. Marryat, pp. 387–390.

18. *Ibid.*, p. 389.

19. *Ibid.*, pp. 382, 386.

20. *Ibid.*, pp. 386–387.

21. Jerry Thomas, *How To Mix Drinks; or, The Bon-Vivant's Companion, Containing Clear and Reliable Directions for Mixing*

All the Beverages in the United States, Together with the Most Popular British, French, German, Italian, Russian and Spanish Recipes, Embracing Punches, Juleps, Cobblers, Etc., Etc., Etc., in Endless Variety . . . (New York: Dick & Fitzgerald [1862]), p. 43. The cover-title of Thomas's book is *The Bartender's Guide*.

22. *Ibid.*, p. 44.

23. *Ibid.*, p. 45.

24. Irwin, p. 76.

25. Information supplied by J. J. ("Pat") Butler, steward of the Junior Common Room, New College, through Miles Blackwell, Esq. (B.A., Oxon.), who enjoyed Trapier's posthumous hospitality as a Junior Fellow of New College.

   There is no unitary biographical sketch of Trapier. The basic facts of his life are recorded in *The History of Georgetown County, South Carolina*, by George C. Rogers, Jr. (Columbia, S.C.: University of South Carolina Press [1970]), *passim.* Trapier was born in 1805, attended Yale College, and became an extensive rice planter at Ingleside, Georgetown County, his lands in 1850 producing 510,000 pounds of rice from the work of 118 slaves. Like many wealthy low-country planters, he maintained also a home in Charleston. Trapier died in 1872.

26. David Ogg, "New College, Oxford, and South Carolina: A Personal Link," *South Carolina Historical Magazine*, LIX (1958), 62.

27. Ogg, p. 63.

28. *The Richmond Enquirer*, May 22, 1860. The poem was published without title in *The Enquirer*. Later in the same year it was printed in *The Southern Literary Messenger* as "Virginia, In Our Flowing Bowls" and appears under that title in John R. Thompson, *Poems of John R. Thompson*, ed., with a biographical introduction, by John S. Patten . . . (New York: Charles Scribner's Sons, 1920), pp. 183–184.

29. Clarence Ousley, "When the Mint Is in the Liquor." The text of this poem, written about the turn of the century, may be most readily found in Hazel Felleman's *Poems That Live Forever* (Garden City, N.Y.: Doubleday & Company, Inc. [c. 1965]), pp. 417–418.

30. MS cited *supra*, n. 10.

31. "The legislature of Massachusetts, which state is the stronghold of the temperance society, passed an act last year [1838] by which it prohibited the selling of spirits in a smaller quantity

than fifteen gallons, intending to do away with the means of dram-drinking at the groceries, as they are termed; a clause, however, permitted apothecaries to retail smaller quantities, and the consequence was that all the grog-shops commenced taking out apothecaries licences. That being stopped, the *striped pig* was resorted to: that is to say, a man charged people the value of a glass of liquor to see a *striped pig*, which peculiarity was exhibited as a sight, and, when in the house, the visitors were offered a glass of spirits for nothing." Marryat, p. 314. A variation of the "striped pig" was the "blind tiger," an expression more familiar to later generations.

32. An exception among the evangelical clergy was remarked by James Silk Buckingham, still another English traveller and a determined advocate of temperance. He told of the personal reaction to the temperance movement of a preacher in Macon, Ga.: "One of [the Hardshelled Baptists'] veteran preachers here is said to have declared from the pulpit that he would never submit to be deprived of his worldly comforts by the fanatics of modern times; and among those comforts he numbered his 'honey-dram before breakfast, and his mint-julap or sling, when the weather required it.' " *The Slave States of America* (London: Paris, Fisher, Son & Co. [1842]), I, 197.

33. Sir William Howard Russell, *My Diary North and South* (London: Bradbury and Evans, 1863), I, 118.

34. *Ibid.*, I, 353.

35. *Ibid.*, II, 267. In his story "The Intestate," published in 1832, James Hall wrote of a fictional character who turned to whiskey to ward off the yellow fever in New Orleans: "I first tried the Sangrado plan; drank water, ate vegetables, and suffered phlebotomy. But I soon found that I could not endure starvation, nor carry on the functions of life without a due supply of the *circulating* medium. I resorted to stimulants and tonics—a mint-julap in the morning, bitters at noon, and wine after dinner." *Legends of the West* (Philadelphia: H. Hall, 1832), p. 132.

36. Douglas Southall Freeman, *The South to Posterity* (New York: Charles Scribner's Sons, 1939), p. 85.

37. Richard Taylor, *Destruction and Reconstruction: Personal Experiences of the Late War . . .*, ed. by Richard B. Harwell (New York [etc.]: Longmans, Green and Co., 1955), pp. 92–94.

38. John Esten Cooke, *Surry of Eagle's-Nest; or, The Memoirs of a Staff Officer Serving in Virginia* (New York: G. W. Dillingham Co., 1897 [c.1866]), p. 102.

39. Clifford Anderson Lanier, *Thorn-Fruit, a Novel* (New York: Blelock & Co., 1867), pp. 31, 35, 57.

40. [William B. Taliaferro,] "The Morning Song of the Mocking-Bird," *The Southern Literary Messenger*, XI (1845), 117.

41. [Fanny Murdaugh Downing,] *Pluto: Being the Sad Story and Lamentable Fate of the Fair Minthe* (Raleigh: Nichols, Gorman & Neathery, 1867), pp. 26–27.

42. *Ibid.*, pp. 28–30.

43. Washington Irving wrote in 1807 that Marylanders, like "their cousins-german, the Virginians," were "much given to revel on hoe-cake and bacon, mint-julep and apple toddy." *Knickerbocker's History of New York* (New York: The Century Co., 1910), p. 201.

44. Betty Wason, *Cooks, Gluttons & Gourmets: A History of Cookery* (Garden City, N.Y.: Doubleday & Company, Inc., 1962), pp. 270–271.

45. *Encyclopædia Britannica* (Chicago [etc., etc.]: The Encyclopædia Britannica, 1968), XXIII, 479.

46. John T. Elson, "Bourbon: America's Brandy," *Travel & Camera*, XXXIII (1970), February, p. 14.

47. Nika Hazelton, "Happiness Is Bourbonland," *National Review*, XXIII (1971), 533.

48. Henry G. Crowgey, *Kentucky Bourbon: The Early Years of Whiskey Making* (Lexington: The University of Kentucky Press [1972, c.1971]), pp. 140–141, 120, 122–123.

49. Lawrence S. Thompson, *Kentucky Tradition* (Hamden, Conn.: The Shoe String Press [c.1956]), p. 31.

50. *Ibid.*

51. Judge Smith's receipt has been printed many times. It is probably most readily available in Thompson's *Kentucky Tradition*, though there the first four sentences of the final paragraph are omitted. The text given here is as it was published by the late Joseph C. Graves as a Christmas keepsake in 1949: Soule Smith, *The Mint Julep: The Very Dream of Drinks, from the Old Receipt of Soule Smith Down in Lexington, Ky.* ([Lexington:] The Gravesend Press, 1949).

52. Carson, *The Social History of Bourbon: An Unhurried Account of Our Star-Spangled American Drink* . . . (New York: Dodd, Mead & Company [1963]), p. 215.

53. *The Southern Punch* (Richmond), I (1863), no. 1 (August 15), 5.

54. Gen'l P. G. T. Beauregard Marching and Burial Society, Membership Card.

55. Helen Bullock, *The Williamsburg Art of Cookery; or, Ac-*

complish'd Gentlewoman's Companion . . . (Williamsburg: Colonial Williamsburg, 1938), pp. 225–226. Mrs. Bullock credits her receipt to "A *Williamsburg* Symposium 1699–1938," obviously referring, not to a publication or scholarly forum, but to "symposium" in its literal meaning of "a drinking session."

56. Harriet Ross Colquitt, *The Savannah Cook Book: A Collection of Old Fashioned Receipts from Colonial Kitchens* . . . (New York: Farrar & Rinehart, Inc. [c.1933]), pp. 168–169.

57. By Will Lampton; quoted in *The New York Times*, December 4, 1934, p. 21.

58. The receipt for an elaborate julep, calling for brandy or whiskey, is given in the best known of New Orleans cook-books:

Mint Julep a la Creole
Julep Menthe a la Creole

Cup of Water.
3 Lumps of Sugar.
1 Tablespoonful of Good Brandy or Whiskey.
The Juice of Half a Lemon.
A Bit of Lemon or Orange Peel.
6 Sprigs of Fresh Young Mint.
A Few Ripe Strawberries.

"Take one large cut glass, half filled with water, add six sprigs of fresh mint, three lumps of sugar. Stir well, till the sugar is absorbed. Add a tablespoonful of good Brandy or Whiskey, and stir well. Add a little lemon and orange peel, and the juice of half a lemon, if desired. Fill the glass with crushed ice, and decorate on top with sprigs of mint. Place a few ripe strawberries on top of the mint, sprinkle lightly with crushed sugar, and serve.

"This julep was a famous offering at the ancient plantation homes of Louisiana. Sliced orange or sliced pineapple is frequently added." The New Orleans Picayune, *The Original Picayune Cook Book: Thirteenth Edition, Containing Recipes Using Wines and Liquors Customary in Early Creole Cookery* . . . (New Orleans, La.: The Times-Picayune Publishing Co., c. 1966), pp. 353–354. The first edition was published in 1901.

59. Harry E. Bowen, *The Mixer* . . . (San Francisco: Select Publications, c.1933), p. 10.

60. *Ibid.*

61. Carson, *The Social History of Bourbon*, p. 215.

62. *Gourmet*, XXIII (1963), no. 6 (June), 43–44.

63. *Ibid.*, XXIII (1963), no. 5 (May), 2.

64. *Ibid.*, XXIV (1964), no. 6 (June), 1–2; XXIII (1963), no. 8 (August), 2–3.

65. *Ibid.*, XXVIII (1968), no. 7 (July), 30–31.

66. The crush-or-not-crush question is confused rather than clarified by the receipts given in *Here's How*, an early post-prohibition manual of mixed drinks by William Campbell Whitfield. Mr. Whitfield gives this for a "Kentucky Mint Julep":

"Put 12 sprigs fresh mint in bowl, cover with powdered sugar. Crush with wooden pestle. Place half the crushed mint and liquid in bottom of a 12 oz. tumbler, half fill with crushed ice, add rest of mint liquid and finish filling glass with ice. Pour in Bourbon Whiskey until glass is brimming full, and place in refrigerator for an hour or so (get thee behind me Satan). Serve with mint leaves dipped in powdered sugar."

This for a "Georgia Mint Julep":

> 4 sprigs fresh mint
> 1/2 tablespoon powdered sugar
> 1 1/2 jiggers fine whiskey

"Place all in large glass, fill with crushed ice and stir gently until glass is frosted. Decorate with mint leaves." (Note that the mint is not bruised in this recipe.)

This for a "Maryland Mint Julep":

> 1 1/2 teaspoons powdered sugar
> Dissolve this in water.
> 4 sprigs fresh mint
> Bruise, but do not crush.
> 2 jiggers Rye Whiskey

"Put these in a tall glass filled with crushed ice, stir until frosted and decorate with some more mint." (This might be called the "Maryland Compromise.")

And this for a "Brandy Julep":

"Use large goblet, fill with fine ice and add 1 jigger Cognac. Muddle several sprigs of mint in a little water and sugar, strain this liquid into the goblet. Add 1 dash Jamaica Rum, stir and dress with fruit and a few sprigs of mint dipped in sugar. Serve with a straw." William Campbell Whitfield, *Here's How: Mixed Drinks*, compiled and ed. by W. C. Whitfield; decorated by Tad Shell. (Asheville, N.C.: Three Mountaineers, Inc., n.d.), p. 23.

67. [William Sydney Porter,] "The Duplicity of Hargraves," *Sixes and Sevens*, by O. Henry (New York: Doubleday, Page & Company [c.1911]), pp. 133, 137–138, 141–142, 143.

68. Elson, p. 14.